Unsymmetrical Body

poems by

Jennifer R. Edwards

Finishing Line Press
Georgetown, Kentucky

Unsymmetrical Body

ACKNOWLEDGMENTS

Publisher: Leah Huete de Maines
Editor: Christen Kincaid
Cover Art: Jr Korpa https://www.jrkorpa.com/
Author Photo: Jennifer R. Edwards
Cover Design: Elizabeth Maines McCleavy

Order online: www.finishinglinepress.com
          also available on amazon.com

Author inquiries and mail orders:
Finishing Line Press
P. O. Box 1626
Georgetown, Kentucky 40324
U. S. A.

Table of Contents

IV. Work Words Do

V. The Want Is Essential

For my family:
those I still have, and those I miss.
Especially Mom, for loving books & coffee talk,
my amazing children, Jaida & Dylan,
and my love, Mark.

I.

Existence, Exodus

I'm Trying

not to weaponize bitterness.
Not to poison or overwhelm when
knocking down doors barely creaking
open or remaining locked.

I'm enabling my tired breath & breasts
to rust & ruin the outdated, overwrought
hinges in our labeled or self-proclaimed
or imposed hallways.

I'm trying to understand complexity, duality,
how a door never swings equally in both
directions, why exits outnumber entrances.
To arrive unannounced, unapologetic.

I'm trying to examine all evidence of affection,
trust gravity in a mouth mid-kiss.
I'm expanding my idea of ownership
to my space and bountiful borders,
all cells & sinew & carnal sound & silence.

I want vastness that motivates.
I need my nothingness acknowledged.

I'm trying to crease kindness & generosity
& listening ears into unforeseen planes
that can't get carried by storms.

I'm trying to recall weightlessness,
be an unsymmetrical celestial body,
a heart beating the world.

Father's Grapefruit

Westerns seeped in while he traced the curves,
crafted swift but tender separations of fruit and skin.
 Strong-armed business suit slice down the middle,
 glottal stop of steel meeting battered board.
 Back bent as the monogrammed R on his
 handkerchiefs below the beige cupboards.

With him, breakfast was never cereal or eggs; nothing without
a proper season or seal, like those disks crystalized overnight.
 When we woke, we found bright yellow oceans,
 sugar slick as ice (I loved to watch him cut through that, too).

He was gone while we savored our sweet suns. Mother orbited
her familiar Formica, her coffee cold and dark as a saddle,
 always reaching with her slightly open robe
 casting shadows on crustless dry bread.

At the Table

sugary morning
tender tongues always need more
dissolve yellow light

Mom Was Always Reaching

into her overpowering purple pocketbook to appease us,

packing and unpacking her mobile junk drawer; a layover of years.
Crudely counting coins, spinning & slapping & sliding
them across counters, pushing pits of pennies
as if she was all in. We rolled our blue eyes.

Cash is king, Dad said. He taught us balancing stacks,
stocks & rebounds, curls of paper off calculators, the sexy suck
of cash in slots, sudden goodbyes with briefcases, final
decisions like a snapping suitcase, *fun money* stashed with socks.

But mom never stopped stooping for gummed up
quarters in Grand Union parking lots, emptied her basic
black change pouch for freezing bell ringers with candy canes,
acted like the bent spine of a thrift store book was enough.

Her dish-cloth damp, spatula-slapping hand opening doors
unannounced, pulling from the bottom when we came up short.

My Father Was a C.P.A.

I wanted to be one too, heavy with knowledge & Diet Coke from the machine, cooped up for hours in a brick back corner office facing the parking lot with the reserved signs reading MJK. I wanted cursive cover letters on creamy correspondence, trails from adding machines on Berber carpets, the math & maneuvering of wealth through accounts & veins all day, pumping and pumping like high blood pressure, like a looming heart attack, all the red paper margins and white columns, reams of paper anticipating numbers. I wanted profit & contractual promises, solid desks with loaded shelves & pictures of old vacations. Our work spaces could connect like hotel suites. I could be a co-worker, a beneficiary of clients & confidentiality & stock trading tips & continuing education credits; inherit cases upon cases with mandatory travel & April overtime & end of the tax season splurges & expensive office parties in Stowe, VT with Charlie Sheen. It seemed like being a small-town lawyer, really, all that important paperwork with mandatory signatures, knowing who could notarize immediately. So many men with suits and ties, hushed family problems, sideburns running back and forth, trimmed facial hair scratching against phone receivers, countless brief emails, lunch meetings on the clock. So much middle-aged importance & impotence, cholesterol through the roof, all living on borrowed family time, their wives trying to take away junk food & secretaries sneaking it in. Always an office birthday to celebrate. Always a bonus when the year went well, and the years always going well. My skirt would billow & flutter & distract while I hushed it with smoothing palms. Nobody would need direct explanations. Voices would be low if I was around. I could finally shut the door being the last to enter, have my name mirrored on the glass at my back.

You Are My Window

—For my mother, always

You are my window opening to reveal the world,
letting in fresh breezes in low, soft whispers
that bounce off the walls of my mind & echo lightly yet
are still distinguished from the harsh noises of everyday life.

You are my window. From your reflection
I see all that I am & through your transparency
all I am capable of becoming.

Cancer Made Grandma Sentimental

—For Doreen Merrill

Grandma asked about the maternity ward constantly,
had me count feet and blankets. Especially
blue blankets. *How many sons bear names today?*
She asked as the oxygen tank worked its
mysticism below her solitary breast.
Then I didn't recognize the woman before me
who worshipped my mother—
her only daughter of seven children,
her sharer & bearer of hardships & housework
& diapers & care for a child who could never leave home &
bail money & coffee chats, who held her daughter up
as one might clutch shiny fruit despite starvation.

Why suddenly blue, after wanting nothing but pink,
the comfort of a softer, pink face that never left?
I didn't think about bearing names or seeing myself
in the face of the dying, but went along
with talk of blue, of toes tiny as pebbles,
of her favorite WWE wrestlers & the terrible
women that cheated on them.

Conditions

Mrs. Slayton never replaced the broken glass, so the history room seemed open and breezy. We could watch heads turn while passing by, her steady words spilling out and echoing off lockers. She was not weird or deserving of mistrust, but tales of her eccentric manners floated through the middle school like the memories of our grandparents who graduated back when it was all granite and freshly cut wood. Originally, a high school worthy of respect. Although I never saw her light up, she seemed to encourage smoking by disappearing behind the tree line every break and beaming her teeth like tiny candles. She gave students their first highs by leaning over to point out Egypt or urge conversation about ethnicity rather than tribalism. To her, life was as simple as the feudal system and she seemed to accept her limited role in our ignorant days as a sort of martyrdom for love of knowledge. She could explain anything in three steps or two opposing interpretations. She examined multiple primary and secondary sources. Her husband once taught geography but became looney. She wasn't afraid to talk of strange episodes taking their toll on her wrinkled face. Since my mother attended every school event and grocery shopped at the same store, she became friends with Mrs. Slayton in ways I still don't understand. My mother hates slang, says conditions have proper names, even classifies in terms of diseases versus illnesses. One day Mom unpacked the plastic bags and said Mrs. Slayton's husband was *schizophrenic* and not looney, just as my uncle was *autistic* and not retarded. I wondered how much mom would smoke if Dad went crazy; how many lighters she would leave around the house if he couldn't work his 40+ hour week and be at the dinner table at 6pm sharp. What I've loved most about my life is how I never had to worry, never was unsure of what might happen because change always seemed beautiful with its constant motion. I somehow felt such conditions didn't apply to us. Dad was always orderly, scheduled, stressed in a nice, professional way; never finding use for words like vassal, honor code, caste. We knew all the proper words, but also not to talk about *private family business.* Our town was made of mouths and rolling eyes.

Inspiration

The first time she read his words was revelation. A flood of feeling better off, the sudden calm of *this is best*, inner rumblings of power & discovery. She sucked up insight through a narrow straw, ecstatic as a hick handling new technology. What wasn't beautiful to her at that moment? What couldn't he master, so much of him arranged on sheets in tight little columns? Every sentence, like a lover's midnight utterance, was oddly familiar. It was like she once possessed those thoughts beneath her tough skin and they had protruded, proud and continuous, onto paper. Yes, everything seemed hers, but more cleverly stated, crafted, gorgeous line by line. It was too late to want anything else, to imagine language had limitations. He had a waiting list. Once she met him nothing changed. Desire magnified. She felt like an octopus, slyly reaching in every direction. She hid affection like candy wrappers at the bottom of the bin, afraid any digging would spark discovery. His words reeked of relativity, human frailty, the burning hum of sexuality skimming below the surface. He was handsome, a muse, all she ever wanted and would work towards. If he was wearing blue, nothing held her attention. His eyes sloped down a page while she read him over, every curve like a whispered promise in sunlight. Two semesters worth of studying him and the towers came down and she learned, relearned, second guessed, circled back to what she thought she knew of memory. *The want is essential*, he declared, *in stories.* And she thought, *in all of life.* Eventually, the obvious. He wasn't hers. Not his own even, only a thoughtful, dreamy presence at the front of the room meant to speak in inspiring tones, raising and lowering his voice, offering his past self (good or bad), the complete self he couldn't help but be, to anyone. She was only beginning then, though much was ending. *How old is old?* she wondered. She was discovering what she wanted, what a girl like her might do if everything actually came her way. Like him she would shape herself and others, turn them into stories, make magnificent masks of language. Like tiny pinatas, people would be placed high and knocked down, satisfaction spilling like sour candy.

Hungerford Terrace, Burlington, VT

Bells from a church I may never enter
echo through the half-asleep street,
the wind like a faint yawn of someone
more physically exhausted than tired.
Their tones seem no longer the results of human hands,
and I cannot picture a faithful old man
mounting stair after creaking wooden stair
to join his calloused hands to fraying rope
in a downward dance to silent counting.
They sound low, steady, certain as a map spread before me.
It is like longing, the way they drag themselves out:
sound offering solace to the night,
bouncing off bare walls of lonely apartments;
so many of us unaware
of how grace reverberates through bone.

Sometime Near Dawn

I woke and found our television
flashing and mumbling
as if half asleep and powerless against
the burning necessity to speak,
like a tumultuous lover
who cannot resign to rest.
The curved arm beneath my shoulders
glowing seductively from those
momentary blurs,
like an ancient lighthouse
still beckoning in universal tongue:
home, home, home.

I'm Not Sure What to Do With This

clown car of a uterus,
tilted angry apparition,
fleshy aborting assassin
rushing and flushing out all life.
The tired tide, disappointed dash
past damaged doors. This sickening
cyclical procession of existence,
exodus.

II.

The Gravity of My Mouth, Or, My Body Brand New

Ceilings No Longer Hold Me

The stark ceiling looms like an angry ex-husband,
touching everything in the room & I am supposed
to teach them to talk, but I hear the roll
of minutes like toys down stairs.

Nothing works like it used to. The kaleidoscope
of color as I shift my contacts reminds me of
another sky barely visible through the natural tent
of leaves brassy, bruised, & brilliant

as I lay on the small hill with pink thumbs
of strawberries that I sucked without
hesitation, before dirty things could hurt me.
Air was lighter & cleaner, absorbing

the dank treasures of the brook & mysteries
of the unfinished cellar. Breathing was more guttural
in Vermont. I learned to speak
in tricking tongues, to melt snow & hearts

one cupped hand at a time.
Fans interrupt in this foreign,
overwhelming heat. I need the haze,
tidal waves of sun and grass at my cheeks

as I roll off course, my body a brand-new catapult,
the final pressure of the wood at my back,
working memory of maples arching in admiration
of the sun. I need the whispering mountain

breeze tickling my ears after climbing out from
behind the leaning garage where a snake's ghostly
skin peeked between granite slabs. Need shadows
creeping toward the metal slide; to blunder back

inside where black wooden cats look down from door
frames and mother stirs her silent, steaming offering.

Three Years, Folded, Blue

Our fingers flame
through final fissures
with solitary static,
scorching silence,
as I return Gram's
ancient afghan.

We agree it should stay
in the (your) family. All this time,
and we still don't understand
what we give away or back
or up. We let our children's faces
tell us how to feel.

Ex-Husband

Again, he steals forgiveness
as if sucking marrow from bones.
At what cost do I give it? My heart gray
as his hair; or some silver, second-best badge.
My body turns over, rising to the surface again.
I wish what was dead would just sink.

What I Ask of the Dead

Spy me on the mountain where I try to breathe you in.
Be sudden and loud as a surprise party. Pain free.
Have your unchanged, mid-joke face
exactly as I forgot to remember you.

Recognize my darker hair, finely grooved face,
the bulging and broken veins of overworked legs.
Don't bother with guilt; that's over now.
Tell me you have learned the things I wanted us both to learn:

perspective hovers above slanted horizons,
intentions become clear as a backlit image,
forgiveness is round and heavy as a ring held to light,
love lives apart from words and signatures.

I ask the dead what they ask of me; nothing
specific wrapped in the language of longing.
I ask the dead what I can't of the living:
what hurts more, the leaving or remaining gone?

Postcard from 2016

The residue of days remained
like the dead, slick skin of lovers.
Facebook memories throbbed like mounting infection.
Campfires were dull and smokey.
I couponed, shacked up
with silence & low expectations.
Adjusted my attitude & furniture & hair color.
Saved & stacked rather than discarded.
Discovered ritualized experimentation
with power tools & a glue gun.
Melted, mended, molded with a matter of degrees.
I let my daughter pull the trigger;
minimized directions to instill
I trusted her instincts. An awkward
formation of transparent soldiers
lined the drafty garage shelf.
Silent wine bottles with backs arched
against petite pickle jars awaited
spray paint, plastic flowers,
mass-produced mantras,
silver keys tiny as pills,
four letter words I barely believed in.
The eloquent, electric blue vase finally
held roses in September
when the smooth driftwood
of my past resurfaced and I
shakily dragged it to shore
like so many disguised treasures.
I pressed past the pale alley of always,
turned my aging face against
the awkward wind of whispered,
empty promises. Held my handful
of glorious moments like a buzzing
lady of liberty clutching her lucid
light, proclaiming
a vague change in plans:
Live,
Laugh,
Love.

I Became Melancholy

—After Lana Del Rey's song Born to Die and Sia's song Elastic Heart

Melodramatic. Which is to say moody. Which is to say mediocre. I monopolized my days with thoughts of prior days. Too much depended on me. I memorialized the living that nearly killed me. I couldn't shower or walk the dog without listening to Lana Del Rey or Sia. My heart became elastic, stretched and snapped back. I made them into the sultry sisters I wanted. They supported my growing obsession with beards and dark-haired men with well-developed muscles that lifted me upstairs, my college hockey jersey pushed up, my new notion of myself as a bendable, beautiful mess. Like a fragile human bird taking little bites, watching for the cage doors to open, always slipping out and back inside unnoticed. I became tinier and tinier, almost breastless; ate only when truly hungry. My hair frizzed and grew like a horse's mane, my children rode on my back. I trotted through town unbridled. Monochrome. Monotonous. Mainly thirsty for cheap wine or new experiences. Sad. To say depressed would be to self-diagnose. Anyone with my advanced level of education knows WebMD is dangerous. To have a diagnosis requires treatment or medicine or (worse) acknowledgement that breeds lifestyle changes. I cleaned and redid flooring. Manic. Even the word maniac involved a man. Wasn't that the real root of all this, the precipitating event, the stressor that continued to deplete my system? Malignant; the creeping blackness invaded the chambers of my heart. My friend from book club called me a drama queen, according to my ex-boyfriend. Although the fact that he's an ex meant something I thought, and he never let me go out often, and he privately texted with her. So maybe that was yet another lie from him. Malicious. Mean. Maybe I should have asked her. No. Some questions have only hurtful answers. So I turned it over and over, like a coin minted every evening. Massive. Maternal. Melodious. I turned on Taylor Swift and the disco ball; danced and shook the sillies out. The kids kept making me laugh.

The Gorgeous, Anxious Girl from Tom Petty's Free Fallin' Video Contemplates Jumping

Nothing is out of place here with my golden locket and hair streaked by Sun-In. My mother is pleased with the *good turnout* for the events of my life. This party, like so many others, is *such fun*, the cake with candles gone, our diets blown. I hover by the quiet fringes of the kidney-shaped pool, listening to Elvis. His voice like Dad's while shaking the ice of his draining glass, like tires on cement making women listen.

Lately a boredom has begun. The malls and clutter can't cure this. I watch others from behind magazines and think I want to be slightly ugly. Prettiness is endless work; scrapes remind me my skin is real. Boys only want one thing and I'm slightly scared of them, their smells and hairy grip, how their anger unzips like a leather jacket. The way they want girls to get right in and push over near their friends, look over waitresses as if the whole world must fill their bottomless cups.

Nobody asks what I want. I was stupid to think someone would write my name in the sky. Still, I search the slanted horizon and take off. The crisp air knows how to touch me, knows I'll return for more. I squint with no clear image of what's waiting to support me, what carefully calculates my landing through the trajectory of years.

III.

Solid Second Chances

New Year's Morning My Son Appears

suddenly, solid as a second chance, asking me to unseal
his sand art kit. I hold his fragile heart, and pour.

I funnel & fill with tiny tools as if hollowness can be flooded
with beauty. Yellow sand lingers like lane markers in our rutted table.

I furiously pack down, seeking some strong,
smooth surface for piling my imperfections.

I consider the close cork of completion, how hurtful
hands & misguided movement might spoil our perfect pattern.

On tiptoes, he spins the glass like a waxing moon
until I take it away to enclose more.

Directions for a Single Mother to Avoid Crying

—Dedicated to the NH Child Advocacy Center

While you wait
for them to tell you if
they think your daughter
was touched more than
she has told you & you
consider words she doesn't
even know she doesn't know,
bathe in the unsettling sea
of tiny hand prints.
A rising rainbow of jellyfish,
surfacing at the ceiling,
unaware of their sting.
Hundreds of delicate,
terrifying tentacles,
outstretched for holding.
Trace them with a sad index
finger, unpolished, bitten.

Know there is no rushing
whatever the moment becomes.
Consider which color she will
press to the probing walls
now the sepia of sorrow
has stained her fleshy heart.
Eat cookies. Somehow   swallow juice.
Color a picture   the turtle   like she
had on her frilly one-piece
a few summers ago.

Dive into the murky shallows
of professional opinions.
Let your swollen lids filter light,
make shadow a temporary home.
Speak nothing of this when they emerge,
while paint is squeezed on paper plates.

She leaves her fuscia prints & selects the softest bunny
that won't leave her bed
until she is almost 13.

Spelling Homework

The teachers, tactful as a parole board,
explained why my *children of divorce*,
needed *additional support for success*.
So I learned to love Mickey Mouse
dancing his hundredth hotdog dance
on the TV to please my son.

She cannot spell Valentine's Day
but remembers the capital letters. It's true,
valentines are confusing. I'm there but I'm not.
I don't see her errors until they stretch
across the page. Five small, similar failures,
the handwriting innocent and terrible.

I don't yet understand this is a disability.
I give basic, unclear directions: sound it out,
keep trying. How can I make her learn?
I am too full of rules. I'm so boring.
Her eyes flit longingly to the screen. I need her
to believe books might save her in ways I can't.
Sometimes my yell is the pressing call to action,
the ugly conclusion. Sometimes it escapes
as suddenly as a dog's reflex to the unfamiliar.

But I don't have it in me tonight.
We are beautiful, tired and helpless
in the pale lamp light. We continue,
copying our mistakes, struggling to stop
what is not yet habit.

The Dreamcatcher

I like to think it was crafted by Native Americans,
full of lore & love. That it kept some bad things
away, as it was meant to the day your father and I,
still wet with spray & sweat from Niagara Falls,
plucked it down like ripened fruit. Another
compromise; chinsy, an affordable, portable memento.
More permanent than echoes of rushing water
that took our voices, making us trust only faces.

It has been up in three houses, two states,
over beds where babies were made & slept
between two radiating bodies, where fires
burned, rekindled, snuffed out again. It
tickled your feet, twirled over your soft,
unspoiled face, helped focus your crystal eyes.

Yes, you may take it down,
place it high above your bed,
add your ancient name in gaudy beads.
Feel the feathers part like short hair through
fingers, thin pillows come undone,
the maze of leather webbing like scarred skin.
Imagine a great-winged bird in flight.

Embracing the Routine

Time for school and work,
I coax. But things have changed.
The day's eight terrible tentacles
will surround me. The youngest
doesn't recognize well intentioned lies
or the dance of worries along a forehead.
He stirs my coffee ineffectively.
He sucks a puddle of sugar off his finger tip.
He says *Kitty is heavy* although
he did not pick her up yet. He calls
for the ancient, cat shaped cookie jar.
Its whiskers are faded,
the porcelain collar chipped.
The last three white beds of cream
dissolve on our sluggish tongues.
Our eyes meet; it is good we got up.

Life is good

Jobs in each state although the old
man's gavel decides which I begin.

Friends who drink martinis, pretend I'm
lovable, let my words rain down upon dark tables.

A man who lets me pull his dark, secretive beard,
is not surprised when I bite his shoulder hungrily.

Children who know nothing of these.

Packing Up

Things here can hurt:
nails missing studs
where we meant to insulate,
carcasses trapped in wanton webs,
scattered gas cans, rusted razors
left over from custom carpet jobs
on lake homes, an awkward igloo of boxes
approaching the garage
ceiling where you added a plywood floor
for storage. The ladder violently comes at me
when I grab the tennis ball string.

I uncover another blue beer can from a trench
of unclaimed tools. This was your gritty escape,
such pathetic protection from the tundra of extreme
temperature, taste, tendencies. Everything freezes here.
We leave nothing to nature. Mice snack on our sad
history, their terrible feet tiny as our lost baby.

Your work gloves awkwardly anticipate return.
They are hard & stained with dried sweat, clumsy
as an unidentified bra in our first apartment.
Rank as the rag resting on the faucet. I consider calling;
isn't there something here you still need?
The breeze yawns & stretches
through streaked, screenless windows.

I sort & sift & pretend I control the keeping.
Haven't I been simplifying? I cleaned the chambers
of my heart all day. I asked what brings me joy.
I squeezed every sponge. I tossed the textured baby
book after stroking the sheep once more.

We had good intentions but we hurt each other.
My fiancé would say we can buy new gloves.
Carry them into our new life. I want

to slip my hands into these virile grooves.
I'll give them to my son when we
get around to laying new roots.

Unproductive

Today I did not write a poem. I picked
four more small oblong potatoes.
Felt their rough eyes sprouting. I picked a fat
nub of a carrot and displayed it on the countertop.
I brought in buckets & the solar-eyed frog & swans
that won't last the winter. I considered next summer,
blackberry bushes I may not plant. I pet my dogs
& let them in & out three times before 10AM.
I combined containers of dish soap
& let my son blow bubbles during his bath.
I bleached the counters, used my magnetic
wand & bingo chips to practice /r/ words.
I modeled by hand like a tongue, like a small boat anchored.
I bought candy. I watered the ivy & removed
any browning bits. I let my son pick berries off a tree;
warned him not to eat them. Decided against
calling my daughter, out with friends again,
because I missed her. At least I put these words
down crudely to come back to when I don't need them
anymore, when this day isn't even a memory.

Easter Without the Kids

We walk the lines of our property
without mentioning the neighbor's lawsuit.
Touch the fence we'll have to move.
You point out globus sacks of frog eggs
stuck to sticks you carefully inserted
between lily pads. I avoid the shadowy
slate tunnel where the snake poked out.
An abundant sky acknowledges us.
We are filled, already.

At the Ball Field on Memorial Day, 2019

Oh, America,
why are you always trying to die?
Why is history written with violent, steady grip?

I may not know you at all beyond your cold corners,
rutted fields, fear of exposing truths.
Even today your need for closure is evident
on chests of medals and scars and tattoos.

You deserve more; you withstand and withhold
until bitterness is the bomb that scatters you.
Your tall order lacks timely delivery.

You are stunning today with corporate sponsorships,
literacy fundraisers, clean uniforms, slick trumpets,
patience on packed shuttles, flags, flashing
lights, & false eyelashes hiding hangovers.

America, I'm slightly afraid
of you. A foul fear rattles my ribs
while I wait for my children
to return from concessions.

I concede, America. You confuse me:
the way we won't or can't take care
of our best, how some stand
but scowl at those who kneel,

how we accept failures of memory.
Why do we release then await return?
How do pleasure & pain have
the same standard deviation?

We aren't completely ourselves today.
We need our pale reflections in surprising sunlight.
All these children and none feel like mine.
We agree too many people are not here.

My America, I still exist
for your approval. I love you solemn
and sorry, remembering the blood that carried
you, the blood you shed and curse.

Oh, America, I want you
to have a home, be a home;
know you can do both.
I want to wipe spit & dirt off your chin.

Hear the fireworks sizzling *there, there, America.*

Admit it, this ball could be a bullet. Please
don't let it be a bullet. My face is a blank flag,
this body an anthem of loss. Can you see me waving,
wanting my world to return unscathed?

I wish my body bigger, your bodies stronger.
You know where I stand, stark & scanning.
Please, meet me here. Please, send
any emoji or misspelled message.

First Teacher's Summer

1.
Guttural breath, grace,
friendly fog melts snow, this heart;
tricky tongues thaw raw.

2.
Sudden spring shower,
flowers gather for gossip
with babbling boughs.

3.
First teacher's summer—
days stretch with fresh promises,
dock creaks its welcome.

4.
Canopy of trees
recalling their central rings;
looking through your hair.

5.
Swinging longer legs;
minute movements of cloud, pond
reeds with dank secrets.

5.
Sky settles the lake,
million movements blend colors;
change so rapid now.

6.
Shabby window up,
leaves and soft chaos flutter;
this world my blanket.

According to My Ancient Dog

—For Maverick

We are not limited by narrow beams of light.
The air is slick & soft, charged with change.
The leash an awkward afterthought,
a loose bracelet on your thinning wrists.

When your face is pressed like that I know
I could run off again, though our best solitude is together.
I can find my way back but not to this moment.
There are things you won't let me lick or rouse or roll in.
Nothing scares me like it used to. The colors & horns
of large trucks have dulled. You pet my nub
tail in apology for sneaking up, or everything.

Our feet leave holes for shadows. The yawning
breeze enters your coat & the dank caverns of my ears
flop open. You peek emerging stars while I
sniff the wildflowers & sneak brassy grass. You must be
recalling the old dirt road, the calf curiously
growing until it blended into the group. I will
pull you through the darkening paved loop
back to the children-
smells of home.

Co-borrower

1
Two names on the mortgage;
One on all correspondence,
Thank you gifts.

My 30-year terms:
I expect more
than signature sexism.

2
mortgage signatures,
singular correspondence.
We pledge new vague terms.

The Nail

On my son's fifth birthday,
I let out my ancient dog &
slam my finger in the sliding door.
Flesh leaving flesh floors me.
Longing's language is guttural.
Annual agony; nothing solid
surrenders silently.

Tell me what won't leave;
how pain stops when my sticky mouth
wants all of it, takes none of it.
My faulty fists clutch & knead,
hide this small ugliness (too)
at my second wedding.

IV.

Work Words Do

Aphrodesia: Upon Seeing Gloria's Obituary 2 Months After Raymond's

Words disappeared like companions; still *aphrodesia* burned in your mouth. We echoed like swearing, researching it on breaks, debating its spelling. This odd new word, inside joke, noun and verb. Like a family name we spoke it without understanding its ghosts: Open wide now aphrodesia. Hand me that aphrodesia. Well, aphrodesia to you too! *Aphrodesia,* you argued, answered, asked. Flat, disinterested, with impeccable timing. The tattooed girls figured you meant sex. They whispered about aphrodesia they had or were going to have. We could not be satisfied. We begged your husband to tell us what it meant. A beloved pet, a pleasant memory, a winding street, a song hummed by your departed mother? We wanted to believe you were becoming your more beautiful, former self. You smiled when you said it; one of your many secrets. That daily warmth, like a fire kindled from the softest wood, was gone too soon. Did you notice the daily visitor with vivid eyes got thinner? He traveled lightly: simple pleasures, soft intonation, crooked fingers, curving lips. His daily pilgrimage reduced. Again, you shared a home. He held you, never uncomfortable with silence or *aphrodesia, aphrodesia, aphrodesia.* Once, he pushed his walker aside as if a younger, jealous man and pulled you to his side, dancing in the glaring afternoon television. He orbited like a pockmarked moon around a smooth sun, lost in worship, faith encapsulated in frailty. He spun your awkward chair like a muscular man holding a ballerina, humming an unrecognizable love song. Your eyes could still find his. You said simply, *aphrodesia.* My knife was cold and shaking. Dark rivers of peanut butter eroded cheap bread. He broke off pieces tiny as petals to feed you. I went home to an empty house and thought aphrodesia, searched again along the abandoned swale of the mattress.

Speech Therapy

I say, "Take your time. It will come."

 I'm the unfit coach on the sidelines,
so far out of the game it's almost hilarious
or sad how I need them to taste success,

want them to see & smell their words,
stick their picks in the ice of their scattered skulls.
I've heard it all: *fuck,* ex-lover's names

in a language they've forgotten. Actors
with sudden script changes, their tongues
pink kites bobbing and adrift.

I make promises I shouldn't:
that the right words will come to their lips,
arriving like beautiful grandbabies,

or prayers at a remembered bedside.
They arrive like sunrise, guests from
a great distance showing up at the last minute.

Welcome. Welcome. I was just thinking about you.

Circumlocution

Is there some substitution that might do? How often are our words
exact? What lifelines can be reached: synonyms, antonyms, letters, sounds,
numbers, functions, categories, size, shape, color, texture, location, parts,
special features? I look to hands & eyes, detect movements, consider the body
in motion, listen for the rise & fall of pitch, wait for functional signs I taught.
Associations are scattered seeds of concepts. Semantic networks connect like

pumpkin vines. Like telephone wires. Faithful fiberoptic cables. Exhausting
neurological travel takes us everywhere. We go without specific direction,
like strangers debating trivial points. As if fresh from jail, or the hospital,
which is another a type of jail. Mouths feeling every movement they can,
pocketing memory in unsymmetrical cheeks. We love when the invisible
tape gives and the simplest message is the fanciest gift. Words coming

like the best birthdays, slowly then all at once.

Pleasantly Confused

He's so cute; can't we just keep him? my employee said.
He was always so happy & kind & we needed him
that long winter. We informally adopted him & almost hourly
he arrived & met us & his wife of over 50 years & talked
about work as an insurance salesman & cow inseminator. He
held her hand while we worked on her wheelchair positioning.
It was probably more because of him that she never slid out. He talked
enough for both of them. Her eyes hinted of recognition occasionally.

*Like a doctor really. I am responsible for thousands. Three dollars
a cow. Sometimes I had to go back and I'd get paid again.*
We worried he sensed our ovulation though none of us needed babies.
He knew when our staplers were empty & what it meant to be busy.

We compared the blues of our eyes in relation to our shirts or the sky;
wherever he gazed if he couldn't get the word. When he wasn't worried
how he'd get home or who would pick up the children, if you asked
how he felt he'd reply: *Fine and dandy, sweet as any sugar candy.*
He told Kyle, *You can use that line son. That is how it's done.*

Her children got sick of calls: getting in her bed, feeding her solid food,
pushing her wheelchair, confusing anxious Alice for her. We worry about
what people can't say. We pay for mistakes we forget we made.
It didn't matter what I said; they changed his room. He looped the square
then napped on our gym mat until we woke him for dinner.
I modified his diet to *finger foods*. He held a sandwich & searched for her
& they lost weight & at meetings I tried to think of how to slow it down.

Cairns at Preschool

They're learning what slides or won't stand, the joy in crumbling creations.
I give them permission I teach them to ask for. We're disappointed

after each crash. Stand back & everything seems smaller. The world shifts;
even now we're in motion & cells are changing. I can't read without

interruption by memory or good intentions. I can't make anything stop
spilling & spitting & sputtering. When they use spinners, I help them put

thumbs down & mean it, breathe through the blur that's a type of focus &
freedom from boring borders. Nobody has enough language, though I

share what little I have. I hope they always push themselves against the
earth & pile imperfections & place pebbles in familial shapes. Though I

don't do it enough. I want them to say *open, please,* and describe the
treasure inside. To believe the world is a box with no lid. Birds swoop &

then leave us, but they're not gone. They recall our reaching hands.
The leaves fall like ripe fruit letting go. Our starving eyes devour color.

The sky reminds us to stay on task. We want to name what's beyond our
reach. I can't say what we need or put it down here for them to pick over

& stack awkwardly. I describe balance by its absence,
building though we know it falls.

I Try to Write a Poem in Which I Apologize for Another

but it's so insufficient & stupid & short
or exaggerated because apologies should be actions.
I make tiny mouths talk about *tomorrow*.

True
Strength

The ant
that lifts 5,000
times its weight
never stoops to roll a
rock from its place, never
heaves a deadly pebble
or broken dandelion head
at a more attractive
insect.

The dark shape
crawls like a phantom,
like air through tiny pores,
a pirate in a wild sea of grass, reading
slanting shadows like a brilliant watch. It
ventures secretly expectant of returning, content to
climb community dirt mounds, pressing circular
body section by *writhing* section into intricate
zigzagging tunnels through damp earth
layers thin as their backs.

Each day
stealing
sweetness to
lug back to the
hole it loved & left,
dodging disaster, limbs
caked in want for
more than a body
should carry.

The Labor of Longing

—In response to the painting Women in Black, by Marianne von Werefkin

We carry burdens like the babies who left us.
We can't measure weight beyond the redness of reality in upturned palms,
the reconciliation of blood that curses and courses
downstream or screams its scarlet stain.

Our bundles sway like the men who left us.
Imagined promises and threadbare clothing curl our backs.
Our hands are cracked birch boats cresting in the cone
of dusty light where the mountains lick the houses.
"Fall and rise," they whisper to the wind.
"Soak or sear?" they wonder without expectation.
So what of the dank scattering; the jealous shushing stream?

Only here our mothers shake loose secrets
and let words feast on fear. Here stumbles are solitary
and our sisters slap away tears because
we are told hope cannot be divided equally.

We cannot own the voices we carry.
Words are labor and loans; and what do we have to give
besides our quick as poison pace and hearts hard as pebbles
where everything is made heavier?

V.

The Want Is Essential

I Pray, Instead, to Mary

Oh Mary, even mothering the Lord didn't save you from
indecision. You were first to wonder *what would Jesus do?*

You wiped your unfair share of spit & holy secretions.
Scrubbed the salt of earth & ungodly grass stains. No animal
or natural disaster evaded His sticky grasp. Outside for eternity,
a mass of reduplicated syllables, crazy as a coastal storm, your boy.

You couldn't foresee conception becoming your calendar. Time trickled
through His (your) lungs. Your belly a folded map of misplaced youth,
a floppy fish of good intentions, silvery gills weighted with secrets.
The pilgrimage along stretch marks more sacred than sexy.

He was different around you. Nobody knew what he was capable of,
how bodies bleed & bend awkward orbits around healing. But who
could you have told, or prayed to? Everyone wanted to have & hold
your child, make Him the man they needed (not a man at all).

Mary, I can't separate poetry from prayer, gratitude from grief. My body
won't believe its borders. Our need evolved into mystery. Love's a
stranger looming above my bed I recall intimately. The expectant sun
emerges mid-sentence, its crippling smile traps (or emits) your brilliance.

I Want to Go to Daycare Too

I want it set up like a Chucky Cheese or an outdated McDonald's with a play place. With colorful alphabet rugs and X incorrectly phonetically associated with a xylophone instead of a fox. With reading nooks full of textured books & art stations. Marked up miniature easels making tented shadows where I let the boys kiss me or I hide to protest some festering injustice about nothing in particular. I want to paint on walls & tables & wherever my hands fling.

At daycare, when I'm hungry, I'll be an utter terror. Even broke girls will want to walk out & forfeit the day's meager pay & drown themselves in coffee dark as the puddles they told us to stay away from. I'll drool & whine & sputter on until they put something in my mouth. Lunch will be chaos and danger, pathetic airplanes crashing at our lips, fluids squirting on wrists, everything rolling to the ground & reappearing, *uh-oh!* I won't throw anything far enough. Everyone will man their stations around us perched on rickety wooden thrones. We can rock & sway & punch & hate our chairs, but we stay until the straps are oddly comforting. At daycare, there's always more food than you can handle, so you just spit up & keep going.

At daycare, everything can be a game. My tongue will touch food first; roll it like a joke, like marbles that fall out when you forget about them. I want to be fed not having a clue what's on the spoon. At daycare, I can taste this secret ingredient of love I hear so much about. I'll make pathetic faces & close my dank cave mouth & sure enough, I'll get peaches again. I'll eat meat without picturing an animal & nothing will feel too heavy. I want to believe I look good in my diaper. I want someone to stroke my double chin & compare my face to a beautiful moon & call me a Gerber baby. If I finally put fingers up to tell my age, I want to be told it seemed like I was born yesterday.

I'll make a new best friend every day mainly based on proximity. I'll judge others based on body language. I want to pull everyone's hair, shriek so loud people jump. I want to be held high & be relieved again & again that I don't crash. I want someone to pick me up even if I fight them. I want to crawl up a leg & be surprised by who it is. I want to get by based on my good looks.

At daycare I want to craft a new language, build my wobbly tower of soft, reduplicated syllables. I want to shove words into misshaped holes not meant for them, where I can rediscover them later like little treasures. At daycare, my pockets hold more & I finger secret acorns & rocks.

I'll have no concept of time. I'll have so much fun I'll forget to use the bathroom. At daycare, sweet release comes sudden as an angry bite & people are satisfied by the mere fact you pooped. I want to get scooped up & ushered away by my posse for what feels like miles across the daycare & be assured.... *nobody noticed* & they planned for this. Wipes clean everything from top to bottom & extra clothes come out of your Ninja Turtles backpack smelling slightly of your dog so you feel relieved & homesick & confused. You can believe the day is starting over again, move on without a care.

At daycare, I'll be almost exclusively in an inviting lap. I want innocent, hairy arms surrounding me. I want my needy head bobbing on the warm ridges of a strong chest, coaxing me into sleep. I want an adventure story, a head & back rub. Someone to gently pinch my squishy bum & squeal in delight. I want to sit all day in one room with my best friends with no cell phones. I want to chill & cry for our own babyish reasons at any moment, talk about each other like we aren't all in the room, yell a little. I want us to be spent & fall asleep together at almost the same time. I want us all rocked together like we're on a party boat & milk drunk & every bottle is empty & we couldn't possibly be expected to sit up anymore.

I want to wake to my mother's slightly hoarse Humpty-Dumpty voice. Frosted lipstick along my cheeks & gaudy stone necklace hovering near my nose. I want to be temporarily blinded by her snow fort smile, wipe the Aqua Net burn from my eyes. I want to slowly recall my other life, have her take me back there, think I'm on my way to something better & the luckiest person at daycare because I'm leaving & never coming back. I want to feel she's sorry & she'll never leave me again. I want to believe too, that we have some choice in the matter.

Dark Horse as Metaphor for My Missed Lover

—In response to the painting Frenzy, by Władysław Podkowiński

I don't say how our unavowed
journey scared us. Our bodies were glossy.
We gripped cast off hopes distinct and curved
as muscles, breakable as bones, between us.
Some connections cannot be shaken off.

I loved the way he took me
when and where I didn't know
   I wanted
until my voice faded to froth.
Breath bubbled at the back of our collective throat.

His barred teeth,
a sieve for warm saliva,
glinted in moonlight.
His eyes were shallow craters
like mother's untouchable teacups.

He was incapable of my lamenting language;
knowing only the urgency of arms at his neck,
the greedy flames of pale thighs surrounding him,
the gross magnitude of love suspended,
the buoyancy of lust before drowning exhaustion.

I can't recall where or why we went, but I was blurry
and beautiful in sheer slips of darkness. Something unlike blood
coursed through him. He was a buzz of instinct and sinew;
frenzy for some secret ripening fruit resting in the distance.
Our hair was woven by sticky wind.

They don't tell you that even a void has volume.
Everything opened up or converged
like exiting a cave,
like reaching into an expressive mouth.
Grip and gumption were my only gifts.

Even closed eyes were lured by the changing
shapes of light's promise. I could slow nothing
with heavy hands or whipping hair. When rain arrives
I still seek his seething eyes through the trees,
I sense the smallness of being carried.

Fantasy in Fever

—In response to the paining Fantasy on Faust, by Mariano Fortuny

The room narrows (expands), moves memory
into (out of) misted corners. The floor is layered lava,
(no) sandpaper, (no) sheet music (but what song?).
The decommissioned battleship floats in its ignorant frame.
There are too many ways to drown.

I avoid fake news broadcasted over mirrors.
The business of days has phased out;
borders are myths though edges are everywhere.
Nothing is crisp or clean or clearly defined.
In shadow profiles face all directions.

Forgive me. Forgive me.
Feverish fugue, the insistent staccato circling back.
The owl's infamous question wondering
who, who remains here among us
(nobody, nobody).

I close my eyes for God's slick oil spill,
generous brushstrokes of oblivion.

Streets Can't Swallow Us

Hunger's just hurt hanging around (don't look).
Anger a wall cracking (except where I strike).
Hope the cleaver (still cutting). Every door's
dank mouth creaks codewords for closing.

Voices clank like cans crazed by wind. See this dark
tongue, slick ship of muscle, stumbling rhythm of
sinew and spit, roaming within dry borders.
See it leave and come back for more.

The approaching dog, with his aching fur & matted secrets,
knows returning. We are spit-out seeds seeking soil, slender
bodies fitting fissures along cement shelves where we hold
ourselves, hang what was already dropped or broken.

I Thought I Knew Everything to Fear

39 years of overheard & self-induced hoarseness, recommissioned fairy tales, hypothetical holes in the galaxy & furthest fields, pricker bushes, the diseased & secretive suckling of ticks, rocks thrown off overpasses, unstoppable fate & forest fires, 13 of anything but especially on Fridays, Nerf bullets near eyes, the vegetable sprayer scotch-taped, witches & why we identify them, weapons with & without triggers, how plastic can be molded into anything, absent or vague trigger warnings, ways my laughter (too) makes me a joke, guilty fever, broken glass, varicose veins, unibrows, how ice (too) seeks thinness & slick invisibility & proximity to granite ledges along the interstate, boredom, dumbing down, the brain's terrible potential, reasons planes won't return a brother, the dizzying myriad of ways cells divide incorrectly into stench, the gravity of my mouth like my mother's, how karma shows up so late it's pointless, eyes crossing at birth or public speaking, childless holidays, loveless nights, poor quality pillows, blood stains or a lack thereof, all kinds of crashing & shattering & darkness, poor measurement of depth & distance & height & weight & time apart, our gross guesstimation of intention, men knowing what you want but not giving it or giving it (all) up, how shedding skin is no protection, jobs that bury you, endless hazards in friendship, the brook's rise angering tenants, how everything & then nothing feels like choices, ways we talk around this, my manic modeling of words & proper verb tenses & social expectations as if they exist anymore, how I wished I warned my younger self, how advice flows sparingly now, how minds & men & money might leave for good. I've been exposed to lead paint & asbestos & toxic plastic takeout containers & weed killers & (unconfirmed) Carbon Monoxide & migraines & masons opening windows while renovating & unnamable fumes at nail salons. Still, I know there's more. This triggering onion with uneven layers, how I cover what isn't essential & pack away soft surfaces, how I foresaw none of this & nothing solid separately silently, another heavy meal of seclusion, the glinting knife & its invisible & countless borders, the drop-leaf threatening release, such precarious & consuming space, consideration of all of this & none of it, my ancient dog seizing again, the shiny jowls of exhaustion, the way I think I know something of loss, the way I can't keep proper distance.

Ode to My Jetted Tub

Praise its empty promises I fill with flesh & filth, how it drowns **good intentions.** Cool welcome though I haven't visited in months & **bring**

nothing. Convincing steam, as if this body is **enough** & scathing hurt of heat necessary. If my body could take more, I'd let it. If the water could

strip me again, I'd wish it luck swirling towards some better future than here, with me. Its persistent porcelain blandness & prominence behind

closed doors, potentially seeping onto everything. It (I) could do more. Not exactly fresh or modern, the motor stutters into starting, clings to every

odor & imposed mark, knows mere age is a victory, slows the drain of skin's memory with hope's stubborn plug. Praise its cold shoulder. The properly

positioned kindness of bubbles. What else allows the full extension of my imperfection? Praise this subtle spring hymn without encouragement or

consolation or feigned understanding. The violence below the surface pressurizes into audible language. I listen without understanding, as if

lamenting is merely rhythm & bone. How amazing, not having cracks, filling to capacity, making a life's work of holding vastness, dreaming depth

that doesn't destroy. Praise saturation, limits, erosion of borders, a body that touches another without expectation, the day gurgling down, the

softening of knots & stumbling out of murkiness.

My COVID Diet Isn't a Diet at All

Why didn't I seize subtle joys like avocado
on an English muffin? Teeth are unnecessary
and crude. I thought internal meant contained,
but it's also malleable, measurable, breakable,
blended. Nobody believes in borders.

What doesn't want to find & push into fleshy ceilings?
Space spreads itself into non-existence.
When is the last time I did only one thing?
At the only island I can visit, I swipe
to a poem that said this, but more succinctly.
Brevity is a gift lost in the mail.
I categorize & color code rejections.
It oddly helps to celebrate failures, too.

It's true, less is more.
I love when we misplace silent phones.
I chew shushing questions,
my mouth murmurs back,
What will I really teach today?
Why is this thick-skinned secrecy,
wedge of forgiving fruit, snowy spring
backdrop of occasional birdsong & distant
snoring *still* not quite enough,
but somehow everything?

I devour everything.

Apocalyptic Movies Are the New Farmer's Almanac

Trigger warnings are insufficient. The plot pressurizes & I
won't give my new husband permission to ever move on.
We consider too many tragedies, the slaughter of self-defense.
There's no world we won't tackle together. We are anxious

bodies of back-alley choices, unsafe angles, secret shadow &
thin skulls. Weaknesses resurface like an overwrought
rowboat as straps of structure loosen. So much sinks
or is carried away. It's a tiny protection, not knowing
which of us will die first. We grind tired teeth, gulp as birdsong

swallows silence. Distant chirps are the harbinger of change;
hope heralds a new water-downed happiness. Each pregnant pause
bears an unimagined life. Short arms reach into religion's river to
rouse or drown. Laws change swiftly, with birth & death unequal
in weight or wonder. Small fingers feel darkness; light seeps through masks.

Horrors hide in silence. Most prefer sound. Some questions can only
be answered in song or scream. Always the nameless is our downfall
and delight. Even in inferno, bones recall the cadence of kindness,
the cool measure of a mouth mid-kiss. Today the tufted titmice &

cardinals & goldfinch entrusted their tender trills & took
our mealworm offerings. They carried secrets in locked beaks.
Such drastic flight, drawn by evolution or experience or exultation
in this absurd sun. If a story saves, who tells it & who listens?
Would we wallow or wade through dank dredges of unrealized dreams?
Who will come for us? Who might bring my love to where I wait,
shimmering in slats of summer light beyond the cadence & canopy?

Why do I not tell him if our languid life runs dry, drink
sparingly this canteen of tears, bring a bruising backpack of
petty, past provisions & move methodically toward whatever
sound you associate with home? Call any kindness kin.

This Body a Bowl of Want

Acquaint, beckon, charm, debate, eulogize, facilitate, greet, harmonize,
illustrate, justify, kindle, lament, mobilize, navigate, observe,
propose, quantify, rehabilitate, self-talk, testify, urge,
validate, witness, x out, yammer, zero in.
What work words do, swirling &
sustaining. Take what you need.

There, there

—Poem using book titles during quarantine

1.
We are water,
waiting,
loud and clear,
   lucky
   introspections,
   headwaters
   toward the end of time,
      range of motion
      the sound of paper
      naming the world.

Some luck,
what the living do—
   body surfing,
   bridge of sighs,
   mountain voices.

The river won't hold you.

2.
Ghostwritten,
dry
testimony
on beauty.

Speak,
strange fit of passion,
white teeth,
beautiful ruins,
black and blue
ladder of years,

postcards,
open secrets.

Words We Need

That's so refreshing
Call me again
You have me
Don't wonder why
Just start over
Sleep on it
Hold on tight
I'm sorry too
Sure why not
I still care
Clock out time
Push over there
Come here closer
Walk your dog
Praying for you
Lay down tracks
On company time
Call me anytime
Job well done
I'm pleasantly surprised
Labs look good
Count to ten
You worked hard
I'll call tomorrow
Don't you worry
It doesn't matter
Tell me again
You can drive
A pleasant surprise
I do care
Seems like yesterday

Stop by later
Another time then
You're never done
Know you're OK
So begin again
Consider me informed
Don't let go
That was fun
Turn that up
I would never
There, there honey
Day by day
Please stop worrying
Thank you again
You and yours
Lets keep going
It's your turn
That smells delicious
Happy belated birthday
I thought so
Try once more
Let me sit
You did it
You look great
Get it out
You're like family
Just one more
You're my person
Sorry about that
I was wrong
That wasn't fair

Let's meet up
It gets better
I'll never leave
Enough is enough
Make it happen
Call me over
I forgive you
Do you remember
Come lay down
But not me
Be right back
One more time
Lets revisit this
That feels nice
You know it
You get stronger
Wow, nice job
Tell me again
Here it is
Scans are negative
Just breathe deeply
That looks good
Justice is served
There's no "normal"
I'll take it
Sing that song
Do it again
I loved it
I never knew
Let's start over
This is free

I Want to Grieve like Chewbacca

Guttural, carnal sound, slick canines,
hooded hair, a smattering of reduplicated
syllables, volcanic vowels elongated
until everything scurries. Everything
rumbling into rupture. Draped in
evolutionary ammunition. Dank throw
rug of revolution. Unmarked grave.
Clutching metal given too late. Rusty &
awkward with affection; too large for
human arms to hold. Useless distress signal.
Beacon of nothing. Rage that won't be
relinquished. Mercy a memory fading
fast, making me move on. No longer seeking
another who looks or thinks like me. Finally
escaping the speckled galaxy of expectation.

This World's a Body of Want

I want a body.
A body I want.
The body   the world   wants me
                            to want.
I want.
I want to make
                            this.
I want to make this world better.
I want
(all) this.
I want to make this world
                            still,
                                        better.
I better want this.
I want to
    be better.
I want to
        better
                    make
                            this world.
Still, the world is better for it.
A world is better
            for wanting.
I want the world still.
The world wants
                    me?
A world wants me to want
            it
                    still   every day.
It's better this way,
            to better the world.
I'll make this better.
I'll make way.
            I'll make it.
                            I'm better!
The world's better.
The world wants

      to get better.
My world's getting better?
The world wants me
      better.
The world must be (always)
        getting.
This must be better.
Must be.
This world wants
      better.
The better body can be a world.
The world wants me
              still.
My body is
     still
           a world of want.

Acknowledgments

The author gratefully acknowledges the following publications or websites where the poems in this book previously appeared, sometimes is different versions:

COVID Spring: Granite State Pandemic Poems, edited by Alexandria Peary (Hobblebush Press, 2020): I Thought I Knew Everything to Fear

FreezeRay Poetry: I Want to Grieve Like Chewbacca

Literary Mama: Spelling Homework

Lucky Jefferson: New Year's Morning My Son Appears

Nepoetryclub.org: I'm Trying (Honorable mention for the New England Poetry Club Amy Lowell Prize, selected by Dzvinia Orlowsky)

Palm Beach Poetry Festival reading: Cairns at Preschool https://www.youtube.com/watch?v=Ctp1XrM9rCc

Poetry Super Highway, 2021 Poetry Contest, 6th place: Mom Was Always Reaching

Portrait of New England: Hungerford Terrace

Snapdragon: I Pray Instead to Mary

The Ekphrastic Review: The Labor of Longing, Dark Horse as Metaphor for My Missed Lover, Fantasy in Fever

The Mountain Review: You Are My Window

The Poets' Touchstone: Aphrodesia: Upon Seeing Gloria's Obituary 2 Months After Raymond's, I'm Not Sure What to do With This (nominated by the Poetry Society of NH for a Pushcart Prize)

Tishamingo Arts Council, April 2021 National Poetry Month series: My COVID Diet Isn't a Diet at All   https://www.facebook.com/104122014516734/videos/324500495967488

4Lines.art: I Try to Write a Poem in Which I Apologize for Another

Jennifer R. Edwards, MS, CCC-SLP SLP (maiden name of Jennifer Jennett) grew up in Barre, Vermont and attended the University of Vermont for B.A.s in English and History and a M.S. in Communication Sciences. She's a preschool speech-language pathologist and writer residing in Concord, NH with her husband and children. Her Pushcart Prize (XLIV) nominated poetry appears online and in or forthcoming at *Terrain, The Remington Review, The Racket Journal, Snapdragon: A Journal of Art & Healing, Literary Mama, Portrait of New England, The Ekphrastic Review, Headline Poetry and Press, Lucky Jefferson, FreezeRay Poetry, The Poets' Touchstone, 4linesart.com, COVID Spring: Granite State Pandemic Poems* (Hobblebush Books, 2020). Her poem "I'm Trying" was honorably mentioned for the 2020 NEPC Amy Lowell Prize (selected by Dzvinia Orlowsky). She was a 2021 Thomas Lux Poetry Fellow at Palm Beach Poetry Festival and received support from Colgate Writers Conference. She curates for Button Poetry. She's active in the Poetry Society of New Hampshire, New England Poetry Club, and Down Cellar Poets. She works tirelessly to empower others with communication skills, literacy, and strong voices for telling their own stories. Instagram: Jenedwards8, Twitter @Jennife00420145 Connect with her and see more of her work at https://linktr.ee/JenEdwards

www.ingramcontent.com/pod-product-compliance
Lightning Source LLC
Chambersburg PA
CBHW021155090426
42740CB00008B/1107